SOLAR SYSTEM

FOR KIDS

CONTENT

Introduction

Composition and Structure

Orbits of cosmic bodies

Planets and satellites of the solar system

Sun

Mercury

Venus

EARTH

Mars

Jupiter

Saturn

Uranus

Neptune

The solar system

The solar system is a collection of planets orbiting a central star. Scientists managed to establish that it is about 4.57 billion years old, and it appeared due to the gravitational compression of a gas and dust cloud. The system is based on a bright star - the Sun, which holds the planets and other objects. causing them to orbit at a certain distance. It is many times larger than other objects in its area of attraction in diameter. An interesting fact: the sun has such a large mass that all other planets in the system make up only 0.0014% of its weight. In the solar system, in addition to the star, there are eight main planets, as well as five dwarf planets. It is located in the Milky Way galaxy, in the Orion arm.The solar system is called the system of celestial bodies, which includes the Sun and many other astronomical objects revolving around it. These are planets, satellites of planets, asteroids and other bodies. The solar system is not unique, thousands of other planetary systems have been discovered to date. The solar system is located in the Milky Way galaxy, in the area known as the Orion Arm. There is still no consensus about where the boundaries of our planetary system should be drawn. Anumber of scientists propose to take into account the influence of the solar wind on interstellar space. Where the wind is stopped by interstellar matter, there is a boundary called the heliopause. The heliopause is about 113-120 astronomical units (AU) from the Sun. However, some astronomers also identify the gravitational boundary of the solar system, or Hill's sphere. It limits the portion of space in which solar gravity dominates the gravity of other stars. For the Sun, such a sphere has a radius of about a light year, or 63 thousand AU.

Emergence

Since the solar system is billions of years old, people can only hypothesize about how it came about. The most popular is the nebular theory, put forward by scientists Laplace, Kant and Swedenborg in the 18th century. It is based on the fact that the system was formed due to the gravitational collapse of one of the parts of a huge cloud consisting of gas and dust. In the future, the hypothesis was supplemented by data obtained from space exploration.Now the process of the emergence of the solar system is described by the following steps:

Initially, in this region of the universe there was a cloud consisting of helium, hydrogen and other substances obtained from the explosions of old stars. In a small part of it, compaction began, which became the center of gravitational collapse. He gradually began to attract the surrounding substances to him. Due to the attraction of substances, the size of the cloud began to decrease, while the rotation speed increased. Gradually, its shape turned into a disk. As the compression progressed, the density of particles per unit volume increased, which led to a gradual heating of the substance due to frequent collisions of molecules. When the center of gravitational collapse warmed up to several thousand kelvin, it began to glow, which meant the formation of a protostar. In parallel with this, other seals began to appear in different areas of the disk, which in the future will serve as gravitational centers for the formation of planets. The final stage of the formation of the solar system began at a time when the temperature of the center of the protostar exceeded several million kelvin. Then helium and hydrogen entered into a thermonuclear fusion reaction, which led to the appearance of a full-fledged star. The rest of the disk seals gradually formed into planets, which began to rotate in the same direction around the Sun, being on the same plane.

Composition and Structure

The main body in the solar system is naturally the sun. It accounts for 99.86% of the mass of the entire solar system. To date, it is reliably known about 8 planets orbiting the star. Of these, the next four are terrestrial planets, and the next four are gas giants. Between these two groups is the asteroid belt, which is called the main one, and beyond the orbit of Neptune, the last gas giant, there is another asteroid cluster, the Kuiper belt. In 2006, a new term was introduced - a dwarf planet. They are similar to ordinary planets, but differ only in that there are other large bodies in their orbit. For 2019, 5 objects received the status of dwarf planets, but, according to astronomers, there may be much more of them. The planetary system also includes satellites orbiting the planets. Some of them, such as Ganymede and Titan, are so large that they are larger than Mercury, the smallest of the planets.

Orbits of cosmic bodies

All planets, rocky asteroids and ice bodies in the Kuiper belt move around the Sun in elliptical orbits in the same direction as the Sun. This movement is called progressive or straight movement. An observer looking at the system from a height above Earth's North Pole would find that all of these orbital movements are counterclockwise. In contrast, the nuclei of comets in the Oort cloud are in orbits with random directions corresponding to their spherical distribution around the plane of the planets. The shape of an object's orbit is defined in terms of its eccentricity. For a perfectly circular orbit, the eccentricity is 0. With an increase in the lengthening of the orbit, the eccentricity increases to 1. Of the eight planets, Venus and Neptune have the most circular orbits around the Sun with eccentricities of 0.007 and 0.009, respectively. Mercury has the greatest eccentricity of 0.21, while the dwarf planet Pluto has 0.25 and is even more eccentric. Another defining feature of an object's orbit around the Sun is its inclination, that is, the angle that it forms with the plane of the Earth's orbit - the ecliptic. Again, of all the planets, Mercury has the greatest inclination, its orbitlies at an angle of 7 ° to the ecliptic, and Pluto's orbit, in comparison, has a much steeper inclination of

17.1 °. The orbits of small bodies usually have both higher eccentricities and higher inclinations than the orbits of the planets. Some comets from the Oort cloud have an inclination of more than 90 °, which suggests that their movement around the Sun, opposite to the rotation of the Sun or retrograde.

Planets and satellites of the solar system

The 8 planets can be divided into two different categories based on their density (mass per unit volume). 4 inner or terrestrial planets: Mercury, Venus, Earth and Mars. They have a rocky composition and a density of more than 3 g / cm3. (The density of water is 1 g / cm3). The 4 outer planets, gas giants: Jupiter, Saturn, Uranus and Neptune are large objects with a density of less than 2 g / cm3. They are composed mainly of hydrogen and helium (Jupiter and Saturn) or ice, rock, hydrogen and helium (Uranus and Neptune). The dwarf planet Pluto is unique - it is a low-density icy body, smaller than our Moon. Pluto looks more like comets or the large icy moons of the outer planets than the planet itself. Its presence in the Kuiper belt explains these anomalies.

The relatively small inner planets are hard surfaces, have no ring systems, and have few or no satellites. The atmospheres of Venus, Earth, and Mars are composed of a significant percentage of oxidized compounds such as carbon dioxide. Among the inner planets, only the Earth has a strong magnetic field that protects it from a hostile environment. The 4 giant outer planets are much more massive than the terrestrial planets and have a huge atmosphere composed mainly of hydrogen and helium. However, they do not have a solid surface, and their density is so low that one of them, Saturn, would actually float in water. Each of the outer planets has a magnetic field, a ring system, and many known satellites. Pluto has no known rings and only 5 known moons. Several other Kuiper belt objects and some asteroids also have their own moons. Most of the known satellites move around their planets in the same direction as the planets around the Sun. They are very diverse, representing a wide range of environments. Io's moon orbits Jupiter and has intense volcanism on its surface. The largest moon of Saturn, Titan is larger than the planet Mercury. Triton moves in a retrograde orbit around Neptune, that is, in the opposite direction from the planet's orbit around the Sun. The temperature on the satellite's surface is only -236 ° C.

Sun

The sun is the main object of the solar system, which accounts for 99.86% of its total mass. It is the main source of heat for the Earth and other planets. On the surface of the star, the temperature reaches 5500 ° C, which is comparable to the temperature at the center of the Earth. However, the Sun's core is warmed up to 13.5 million degrees. The extreme temperature and pressure in the center of the luminary create conditions for thermonuclear fusion, which provides energy to the entire solar system.

 Our star consists mainly of hydrogen (73.5%) and helium (24.9%), the rest of the elements account for about 1%. However, due to thermonuclear fusion, the chemical composition of the Sun changes. The hydrogen gradually burns out, and helium is formed in its place. In 5 billion years, when the fuel for a thermonuclear reaction runs out, the star will dramatically increase in size and possibly engulf the Earth.

The sun is a huge ball of hot gas with an estimated diameter of 1.392 million km. It is 109 times the diameter of our planet. The star represents 99.87% of the total mass of the solar system. From Earth it appears that the light is yellow, but this is an illusion associated with the influence of our planet's atmosphere on sunlight. In fact, the sun emits an almost white light. The sun is one of hundreds of billions of stars in the Milky Way galaxy. The closest star to the Sun is Proxima Centauri, 4.24 light years away. For comparison - the distance from Earth to the Sun, taken as an astronomical unit (AU), sunlight passes in just 8.32 minutes. According to the astronomical classification, the Sun belongs to the type of "yellow dwarfs". This means that it is not that big compared to the size of the other stars, but that it shines bright enough. Our star is among 15% of the brightest stars in the Milky Way. At the same time, there are stars in the galaxy whose radius exceeds the solar one by 2000 times! The source of heat emitted by the star is thermonuclear reactions. In the center of the sun, hydrogen atoms merge with each other, resulting in a helium atom and some energy.

This reaction is called the proton-proton cycle, it represents about 98% of the energy generated by the light. However, other reactions also take place, in which elements such as helium, carbon, oxygen, neon and silicon "burn", and metals (iron, magnesium, calcium, nickel) and other elements (sulfur) are formed. All of these processes are called stellar nucleosynthesis. The influence of the Sun on the surrounding celestial bodies is enormous. The solar wind (particles of matter emitted by a star) dominates in interplanetary space at a distance of up to 100-150 AU.

from the sun. It is believed that the gravity of our star determines the orbits of bodies located even at a distance of a light year from it (in the Oort cloud). The Sun itself also rotates on its axis. Since it is composed of gas, different layers of it rotate with different angular velocities. If in the equatorial region the orbital period is 25 days, it increases at the poles to 34 days. Additionally, recent research shows that the inner regions rotate much faster than the outer shell.

The age of the Sun is estimated by scientists at 4.5 billion years. It was formed from a cloud of gas and dust, which was gradually compressed under the influence of its own gravity. From the same cloud, planets and almost all other objects in the solar system arose. When the density in the center of the collapsing cloud, and with it the temperature and pressure, rose to critical values, a thermonuclear reaction began - this is how the Sun lit up.

In the course of thermonuclear reactions, the mass of the Sun gradually decreases. Every second, 4 million tons of solar matter is converted into energy. At the same time, the star is warming up. Every 1.1 billion years, the sun's brightness increases by 10%. This means that earlier the temperature on Earth was much lower than now, and Venus may have had liquid water or even life (now the average temperature on the surface of Venus is 464 ° C).

In the future, the brightness of the Sun will increase, which will lead to an increase in temperature on Earth. In 3.5 billion years, the brightness of the star will increase by 40%, and the conditions on Earth will be the same as on Venus.

On the other hand, Mars will also warm up and become more livable. Thus, in the course of the evolution of the star, the so-called "habitable zone" is gradually moving away from the Sun. Gradually, due to the burning out of hydrogen, the core will decrease in size, and the entire star as a whole will increase. In 6.4 billion years, the hydrogen in the core will run out, the radius of the star at this moment will be 1.59 times larger than the modern one. Over the course of 700 million years, the star will expand to 2.3 modern radii. Further, an increase in temperature will lead to the fact that thermonuclear reactions of hydrogen combustion will start no longer in the core, but in the envelope of the star. Because of this, it will expand dramatically, and its outer layers will reach modern earth's orbit. However, by that time the star will have lost a significant part of its mass (28%), which will allow our planet to move to a more distant orbit. The sun during this period of its life, which will last 10 million years, will be a red giant. Then, due to the temperature rise in the core up to 100 million degrees, an active reaction of helium combustion will begin there - a "helium flash". The radius of the star will be reduced to 10 modern radii. It will take about 110 million years for helium to burn out, after which the star will expand again and become a red giant, but this stage will last for 20 million years. Due to the pulsations associated with changes in the Sun's temperature, its outer layers will separate from the core and form a planetary nebula. The core itself will turn into a white dwarf - an object whose size will be comparable to the size of the Earth, and the mass will be equal to half of the modern solar mass. Further, this dwarf, consisting of carbon and oxygen, will gradually cool down. There will be no thermonuclear reactions in the white dwarf, so over time (over tens of billions of years) it will turn into a black dwarf - a cooled dense mass of matter. This is where the evolution of the Sun will end.

Mercury

Mercury: the first planet from the Sun and the smallest planet in the Solar system. This is one of the most extreme worlds. Received his name in honor of the messenger of the Roman gods. It can be found without the use of equipment, therefore, Mercury has been noted in many cultures and myths. But this is also a very mysterious object. You can observe the morning and evening in the sky, and the planet itself will have its own phases. The planet closest to the Sun is also the Smallest in the system. Its radius is only 2440 km. It got its name in honor of the god of trade, Mercury. Its surface is gray, which is why many compare it to the moon. The planet does not contain satellites, and due to strong solar winds, its atmosphere is almost completely discharged. With a radius of 2440 km and a mass of 3.3022×10^{23} kg, Mercury is considered the smallest planet in the Solar system. By size it reaches only 0.38 earth. It is also determined by the parameters of some satellites, but by density it stands at the second place after the Earth - 5.427 g / cm3. The lower photo shows a comparison of the sizes of Mercury and Earth.

The description of Mercury is not complete without a story of exploration. This planet is accessible for observation without the use of instruments, so it appears in ancient myths and legends. The first records are found in the Mule Apin tablet serving as Babulonian astronomical and astrological documents. These observations were made in the 14th century BC. and talk about the "dancing planet" because Mercury is moving the fastest. In ancient Greece it was called Stilbon (translated as "shine"). He was the Olympe's messenger. Then the Romans adopted this idea and gave the modern name in honor of their pantheon. Ptolemy in his works repeatedly mentioned that the planets are able to pass in front of the Sun. But he did not note Mercury and Venus as examples, as he considered them too small and invisible. The Chinese called it Chen Xin ("Clock Star") and associated it with water and northern orientation. Moreover, in Asian culture such an idea of the planet is still preserved, which is even registered as the 5th element. For the

Germanic tribes, he had a link with the god Odin. The Mayas saw four owls, two of which were responsible for the morning and the other two for the evening. One of the Islamic astronomers wrote about the geocentric orbital path in the 11th century. In the 12th century, Ibn Bajya noted the transit of two tiny dark bodies in front of the Sun. Most likely, he saw Venus and Mercury. The Indian astronomer Kerala Somayagi in the 15th century created a partial heliocentric model where Mercury circled the Sun. The first view through a telescope falls on the 17th century. Galileo Galilei did it. He then carefully studied the phases of Venus. But his device didn't have enough power, so Mercury was left without attention. But the transit was noted by Pierre Gassendi in 1631. The orbital phases were noticed in 1639 by Giovanni Zupi. This was an important observation because it confirmed the rotation around the star and the accuracy of the heliocentric model. More precise observations in the 1880s. Provided by Giovanni Schiaparelli. He thought the orbital journey would take 88 days. In 1934, Eugios Antoniadi created a detailed map of the surface of Mercury.

The composition of Mercury is 70% pre-made to metal and 30% silicate materials. It is believed that its core comprises approximately 42% of the total volume of the planets (Earth has 17%). Inside lies a core of melted iron, surrounded by a silicate layer (500-700 km). The surface layer is a crust with a thickness of 100-300 km. On top of that, you can notice a huge number of ridges, which stretch for kilometers.

-A year in Mercury lasts only 88 days.One sunny day (between noontime) takes 176 days, and a side day (rotational speed) - 59 days. Mercury is endowed with the largest orbital eccentricity, and the distance from the Sun is 46-70 million km.

- This smallest planets in the Mercury system are among the five planets that can be found without using the tools. At the same time, it is located at 4879 km.

- Costs on the second place in terms of density Each cm 3est is assigned an indicator of 5.4 grams. Ho the Earth stands in the first place, because Mercury is predominantly heavy metals and mountainous rocks.

-There are wrinkles When the iron planetary core is back and pity, the superficial layer is covered with wrinkles. They can stretch out hundreds of miles.

-Get a melted core Researchers believe that the ferrous core of Mercury is able to stay in a melted state. Usually, in small planets, it quickly loses heat. But now they think that it replaces gray, which reduces the temperature of melting. The core contains 42% of the planned volume.

-At the second place, according to the toughness, although the Benera survives further, but its superiority stably maintains the highest surface temperature of the air source. The day side of the Mercury is heated at 427 ° C, and at night temperature drops to -173 ° C. The planet is devoid of an atmospheric layer, therefore it is not able to provide an even distribution of heat.

-The best cut-off plan Geological processes help planets to renew the surface layer and smooth out minor scars. Ho Mercury is deprived of such an opportunity. All of his critics are among artists, writers and musicians. Shock formations exceeding 250 km in diameter are called basseins. The largest is the Plain of Heat, stretching for 1550 km.

-He was visited only by two apparatuses of Mercurii, who are too close to the Sun. It flew around Mapiner-10 three times in 1974-1975, having removed a little less than half of the surface. In 2004, Messenger departed there.

Venus

The second planet from the Sun, is named after the ancient Roman goddess of love. Distinctive features are the absence of natural satellites and the high content of carbon dioxide in the atmosphere. The radius of Venus practically coincides with that of the Earth: 6051 km, which is only 5% less. Because of this, the planets are called "sisters." However, outwardly Venus is very different, representing a milky ball. The surface is almost entirely composed of solidified lava with rare meteorite craters.

People in ancient times knew about her existence, but they mistakenly assumed that there were two different objects in front of them: morning and evening stars. It is worth noting that they officially began to perceive Beneru as a single object in the 6th century BC. BC, but still in 1581 BC. e. There was a Babylonian table, where the true nature of the planet was adequately explained. For many Benera became the embodiment of the goddess of love. The Greeks named after Aphodites, and for the Romans the morning appearance became Lucifer. In 1032, Avicenn first observed the passage of Venus in front of the Sun and realized that the planet is located closer to the Earth than the Sun. In the 12th century, Ibn Bajay found two black dots, which were later explained by the transits of Venus and Mercury. In 1639, Jeremiah Horrocks oversaw the transit. Galileo Galilei at the beginning of the 17th century used his instrument and noted the phases of the planet. This was an extremely important observation, which indicated that Venus circled the Sun, which means Copernicus was right. In 1761, Mikhail Lomonosov discovered the atmosphere of the planet, and in 1790, Johann Schroeter noted it. The first serious observation was ruled by Chest Lyman in 1866.

Around the dark side of the planets, a full light ring was marked, which again indicated the presence of the atmosphere. The first UV survey was performed in the 1920s. Spectral observations were carried out on the rotation speed. Since the Sleifer tried to determine the additional displacement. But when he couldn't get it away, he began to guess that the plan was making the revolutions too slowly. More so, in the 1950s. realized that we have to do with a retrograde rotation. Radiolocation was used in the 1960s. and got close to the present-day rotation indicators.

About the details, like Mount Maxwell, could speak thanks to the Aresibo Observer.

VENUS is located between us and the Sun, then it comes to the Earth near all the planes - 41 million km. This happens every 584 days. The orbital path takes 224.65 days (61.5% of the earth).

In terms of its dimensions, it is the closest to the Earth, therefore it is called the "sister of the Earth". The radius of the planet is 6050 km, which is 95% of the Earth's radius. The mass of Venus is 18.5% less than that of Earth. The distance from Venus to the star ranges from 107.5 to 108.2 million km. Moreover, it is hotter on the surface of Venus than even on Mercury. The average temperature reaches 477 ° C, while its fluctuations are insignificant. Such a high figure is associated with a very dense atmosphere, consisting of 96% carbon dioxide. The density of the atmosphere is so high that the surface pressure reaches 93 atm. If Venus had the Earth's atmosphere, then the temperature on it would not exceed 80 ° C. Venus has no satellites, but there is a theory that earlier Mercury was such.

-A day lasts more than a year. The axis of rotation (a side-by-side day) takes 243 days, and the orbital path takes 225 days. The sunny day lasts 117 days.

-Turning in the opposite direction VENUS is retrograde, that is, it turns in the opposite direction. Possibly, in the past there was a collision with a large acteroid. It also differs in the absence of satellites.

-The second place in the sky is bright. For the earthly observer, only the Moon is brighter than VENUS. With a great from -3.8 to -4.6, the planet is so bright that it is shown periodically in the middle of the day.

- Atmospheric pressure 92 times greater than the ground, although by the size of the slopes, but the surface of the beer is not such a short one, as the power of the engine is dense. The pressure on its surface is comparable to what is felt at great depths.

- VENUS is a terrestrial area The difference in their diameters is 638 km, and the beer mass reaches 81.5% ground. They also follow the structure.

- Called the Morning Star and Evening Star The ancients believed that they had two different objects before them: Lucifer and Vesper (among the Romans). The point is that its orbit exceeds that of the Earth, and the planet appears at night or by day. It was described in detail by the Maouas in 650 BC.

- The hottest planet The planet's temperature rises to 462 ° C. Venus does not have a remarkable axial inclination and therefore lacks seasonality. The dense atmospheric layer is made of carbon dioxide (96.5%) and retains heat, creating a greenhouse effect.

-The study was completed in 2015. In 2006, the VENUS-Express device was sent to the plan, which was sent to its opbit. Initially, the mission lasted for 500 days, but then it was extended until 2015. I managed to find more than a thousand volcanoes and volcanic centers with a distance of 20 km.

- The first mission was assigned by the CCCP. In 1961, the Soviet probe of Benera-1 was sent to VENUS, but the contact was quickly broken. The same thing happened with the American Mapiner-1. In 1966, the CCCP managed to empty the first device (VENUS-Z). It was possible to take a look at the surface, hidden behind a thick acidic haze. Advance in research retired with the advent of radio graphic mapping in the 1960s. It is believed that in the past the plan was possessed by oceans, which were consumed due to the rise in temperature.

Previously, it was extremely difficult to see the surface of Venus, as the view was obscured by an incredibly dense atmospheric haze, represented by carbon dioxide with small mixtures of nitrogen. The pressure is 92 bars and the atmospheric mass is 93 times that of the Earth. Let's not forget that Venus is the hottest of the solar planets. The average is 462 ° C, which is stable at night and during the day. It all depends on the presence of a huge amount of CO 2, which forms a powerful greenhouse effect with clouds of sulfur dioxide. The surface is characterized by isothermality (does not affect temperature distribution or changes at all). The minimum inclination of the axis is 3 °, which also prevents the appearance of seasons. Temperature changes are only observed with altitude.

EARTH

The third planet from the Sun, the only one with large territorial areas filled with water. Due to favorable climatic conditions and sufficient resources, it is the only source of life in the solar system. The radius of the planet is 6378 km.

The homeland of humanity. The distance from it to the Sun ranges from 147 to 152 million km. The average value of this value is 149.6 million km and is used in astronomy as a unit of measurement for distances - an astronomical unit (AU). The average radius of the Earth is 6371 km, and the mass of our planet is estimated at 5.97 x 1024 kg.

The Earth is distinguished from the terrestrial planets by the presence of a very large satellite - the Moon, with a radius of 1737 km.

-The rotation slows down gradually For earthlings, the whole process of slowing down the rotation of the axis occurs almost imperceptibly - 17 milliseconds per 100 years. But the nature of speed is not uniform. For this reason, there is an increase in the length of the day. In 140 million years, a day will last 25 hours.

-Earth was believed to be the center of the universe Ancient scientists could observe celestial objects from the position of our planet, so it seemed that all objects in the sky were moving relative to us, and we stayed at one given moment. As a result, Copernicus stated that the Sun (the heliocentric system of the world) is at the center of everything, although now we know that this does not correspond to reality, if we take the scale of the Universe.

-With a strong magnetic field Earth's magnetic field is created by a rapidly rotating nickel-iron planetary node. The field is important because it protects us from the influence of the solar wind.

-Has a companion If you look at the percentage, then the Moon is the largest satellite in the system. But in reality, it is the 5th largest.

-The only planet not named after a deity Ancient scientists named the 7 planets in honor of the gods, and modern scientists have followed the tradition in discovering Uranus and Neptune.

- First in density Everything is based on the composition and the specific part of the planet. Thus, the node is represented by metal and bypasses the crust in density. The average density of the earth is 5.52 grams per cm^3 .

The Earth has plate tectonics. The question of the existence of life elsewhere than on Earth remains open ... Among the planets of the terrestrial group, the Earth is unique (mainly because of the hydrosphere). Earth's atmosphere is radically different from other planets - it contains free oxygen ... Earth has a natural satellite - the

Moon, the only major satellite of the terrestrial planets in the solar system.

Human impacts on our planet: The data clearly indicates that our climate is changing rapidly and that almost all of the change is the result of human activity. This is not the first time that humans have dramatically changed their environment. Some of the biggest changes were caused by our ancestors, before the development of modern industrial society.

50,000 years ago, much of the planet was home to large animals of the genus which now only survive in Africa. The plains of Australia were occupied by giant marsupials such as diprododon and zygomaturus, the size of present day elephants, and a species of kangaroo that stood 3m tall. North America and North Asia have played host to mammoths, saber-toothed tigers, masto dons, giant sloths, and even camels. The islands of the Pacific Ocean were teeming with large birds and vast forests covered what parts of Europe and China are now cultivated lands. Early human hunters killed many large mammals and marsupials, early farmers cut down most forests, and Polynesian expansion across the Pacific doomed the large bird population.

For most of human history, environmental transformation, marked primarily by deforestation and agriculture, has remained relatively localized. But everything changed in the 20th century, with the intensification of industrial activity that began a century earlier.

The effects are now being felt on the chemical composition of the atmosphere, soil and water, as well as on the fate of many other living species. A new, even larger mass extinction is underway today due to rapid climate change induced by human activities. Unique, at least in the solar system, and as far as we can know, the fate of a planet - our planet - no longer depends on astronomical and geological necessities alone. It is the exercise of collective choices and individual responsibilities. To account for the global impact of human activities on the environment, researchers have proposed to give the name of the Anthropocene = human era, at the present time, which began when human activities began. had a significant global footprint. Although not an officially approved term, the concept of the Anthropocene is useful in expressing that we humans are now the dominant factor in changes taking place in the atmosphere and in the world. Ecology of our planet. This recent awareness gave birth to the concept of sustainable development, which now places the development of human civilizations within the framework of the economy of the Earth's resources and respect for its balances.

Mars

Mars is the fourth planet from the Sun and the most posed one on Earth in the Solar system. We know our community also by the second name - "Red Planet". He received his name in honor of the God of war among the Romans. Deal in its red color, created by iron oxide. Every few years the plane is spread out close to us and it can be found in the night sky.

Its periodic manifestation is due to the fact that the planet was displayed in many myths and legends. And the external menacing appearance became the reason for the fear before the plan. Let's find out more interesting facts about Mars.

Mars is smaller than Earth and Venus (0.107 land mass). Similar to our planet in its structure. Its radius is twice that of the Earth and its mass is an order of magnitude less. It has an atmosphere composed mainly of carbon dioxide with a surface pressure of 6.1 mbar

(0.6% of the Earth). On its surface there are volcanoes, the largest of which, Olympus, exceeds all terrestrial volcanoes in size, reaching an altitude of 21.2 km. Rift depressions (Mariner valleys), as well as volcanoes, testify to ancient geological activity, which, according to some sources, has continued even over the past 2 million years. The red color of the surface of Mars is caused by the large amount of iron oxide in its soil. The Martian year is twice as long as the Earth year, but a day is almost the same length. Mars is richer than the first two planets, having two satellites: Phobos and Deimos, translated from the Greek as "fear" and "horror". They are small rocks, very similar to asteroids.

Earthlings have long observed the Red Neighbor, as the planet Mars can be found without the use of tools. The first records were made in ancient Egypt in 1534 BC. e. They were already familiar with the retrograde effect at the time. It's true for them, Mars was a weird star, whose movement was different from others. Even before the advent of the Neo-Babulonian Empire (539 BC), planetary positions were regularly recorded. People noticed changes in movement, light levels, and even tried to predict where they would go. In the 4th century BC. Aristotle noticed that Mars was hiding behind the Earth's satellite during the occlusion period, which indicated that the planet was located further than the Moon. Ptolemey decided to create a model of the whole Blessed one, which would be transformed in a planetary motion.

He assumed that there are spheres inside the plan, which are also guaranty for the relief. It is known that the ancient Chinese also knew about the planet in the 4th century BC. e. The diameter was estimated by Indian researchers in the 5th century BC. e. Model Ptolemeya (geotsentpicheckaya cictema) cozdavala mnogo ppoblem, Nr ona octavalac glavnoy to 16-th veka, kogda ppishel Kopepnik co cvoey cxemoy, Where in tsentpe pacpolagaloc Colntse (geliotsentpicheckaya cictema). His ideas supported Galileo Galilei's observations in the new TV. All of this was possible to calculate the daily parallax of Mapca and remove to it. In 1672, the first measurements were taken by Giovanni Caccini, but his equipment was weak. In the 17th century, Parallax uses Quiet Brague, after which it is corrected by Johannes Kepler. The first Mapca was introduced by Christian Huygens. In the 19th century, you managed to increase the permissibility of devices and to examine the characteristics of the Martian surface. Thanks to this, Giovanni Schiapapelli created the first detailed map of the Red Planet in 1877. It also displayed channels - long straight lines. Later they realized that this was only an optical illusion. The card gave Percival Lowell an opportunity to create an observatory with two powerful televisions (30 and 45 cm). He wrote many articles and books on the subject of Mapca. Channels and seasonal changes (reduction of polar caps) have given us ideas about Marcians. And even in the 1960s. continued to write research on this topic.The red planet was named after the god of war. It is the last, fourth planet in the Earth group of the Sun. Mars has an atmosphere, but it is heavily discharged, and the pressure on the surface is 160 times lower than on Earth. The temperature on the planet varies from − 140 ° C to + 20 ° C.

Mars has two natural satellites - Phobos and Deimos. There are ice caps in the polar regions of the planet. It is believed that billions of years ago Mars might have had rivers and seas, but over time they dried up. The red planet is expected to be the first to be visited by humans in the future. It could happen already in the 21st century.The "red" planet is the most distant from the Sun, belonging to the terrestrial group. It is also considered the smallest after Mercury. Its radius is 3396 km. The surface consists mainly of sandy and earthen reliefs, divided into light and dark areas, called continents and seas, respectively. In the 21st century, Mars is of great interest to scientists. Since the planet is in relative reach, rovers are regularly sent to it to collect data.

-Mars and Earth have a similar surface mass : The red planet covers only 15% of the volume of the Earth, but 2 / 3 of our planet is covered with water. Martian gravity is 37% of that of Earth, which means your jump will be three times higher.

-At the highest mountain in the system : Mount Olympe (the highest in the solar system) stretches 21 km and covers 600 km in diameter. It took billions of years to form, but lava flows suggest the volcano may still be active.

-Only 18 Missions Completed With Success : About 40 space missions were sent to Mars, including simple overflights, orbital probes and rover landings. The latter included the device Curiosity (2012), MAVEN (2014) and Indian Mangalyan (2014). Also in 2016, ExoMars and InSight arrived.

-The Biggest Dust Storms : These weather disasters can last for months and cover the entire planet. The seasons become extreme because the elliptical orbital path is extremely elongated. At the point closest to the southern hemisphere, a short but warm summer sets in, while the north plunges into winter. Then they change places.

-Martian debris on Earth : Researchers were able to find small traces of the Martian atmosphere in meteorites that have come down to us. They swam in space for millions of years before they reached us. This made it possible to conduct a preliminary study of the planet even before the launch of the vehicles.

-The name comes from the god of war in Rome : In ancient Greece, they used the name of Arès, who was responsible for all military actions. The Romans copied almost everything from the Greeks, so they used Mars as their counterpart. The bloody color of the object served as such a trend. For example, in China, the red planet was called a "fire star". Formed from iron oxide.

- There are traces of liquid water Scientists are convinced that for a long time the planet Mars had water in the form of ice deposits. The first signs are streaks or dark spots on the crater walls and rocks. Considering the Martian atmosphere, the liquid must be salty so as not to freeze and evaporate.

-While waiting for the ringtone to appear in the next 20 to 40 million years, Phobos will come dangerously close and be torn apart by planetary gravity. Its debris will form a ring around Mars that can last for hundreds of millions of years.

Jupiter

Due to its scale, the planet could be found in the sky without instruments, so they had known of its existence for a long time. The first records appeared in Babulon in the 7-8 century BC. Ptolemy in the 2nd century created his geocentric model, where he deduced an orbital period around us - 4332, 38 days. This model was used in 499 by the mathematician Ariabhata, and received a result of 4332.2722 days. In 1610, Galileo Galilei used his instrument and was able to see the gas giant for the first time. I noticed 4 bigger satellites near it. This was an important point because it supported the heliocentric model.

A new telescope in the 1660s used by Cassini, who wanted to study the light spots and streaks of the planet. He discovered that in front of us was a flattened spheroid. In 1690 he was able to determine the period of rotation and the differential rotation of the atmosphere.

Details of the big red spot were first described by Heinrich Schwabe in 1831. In 1892, the fifth moon was observed by E.E. Bernard. It was Almatea, which was the last satellite to be discovered during the visual investigation.

The absorption bands of ammonia and methane were studied by Rupert Wildt in 1932, and in 1938 he followed three long "white ovals". For many years they remained separate formations, but in 1998 two merged into one object, and in 2000 absorbed the third.

The radio telescopic investigation began in the 1950s. The first signals were picked up in 1955. These were bursts of radio waves corresponding to the planetary rotation, which made it possible to calculate the speed. Later, researchers were able to deduce three different types of signals: decametric, decimeter and heat emissions. The first ones change together with rotation and are based on the contact of Io with a planetary magnetic field. Decimetric cells appear from the toophase equatorial belt and are generated by cyclonic emissions of electrons. And then it is formed by atmospheric heat.

Jupiter charmed observers for another 400 years ago, when he was removed to look in the first televisions. This is a beautiful gas giant with closed clouds, a mysterious spot, a family of satellites and a lot of features. Most of all he is impressed by the masts. According to the indices of mass, volume and area of the planet, it occupies an honorable first place in the Solar system. Even ancient people knew about its existence, therefore Jupiter was marked in many cultures.

Jupiter is named after the ancient Roman god of the sky, which is essentially similar to the Greek Zeus. It is the largest planet in the solar system. It is about 2.5 times heavier than all other planets orbiting the sun. Jupiter is a gas giant. This means that it does not have a solid surface like Earth or Mars. The bulk of the planet is the atmosphere. At great depths, due to high pressure, gases turn into liquid, so that deep in Jupiter there should be an ocean of hydrogen, but the boundary between it and the atmosphere is not clear. Deeper still, hydrogen can be solid. Jupiter is known for a huge number of satellites, of which there are at least a hundred. Of these, the so-called Galilean satellites (Io, Ganymede, Europa and Callisto), discovered back in

1610, stand out. These were the first satellites discovered by mankind after the Moon.

The largest planet in the solar system. Its radius is 69912 km, which is almost 20 times the earth's. Scientists cannot yet accurately determine the composition of the planet, only it is known that there is more xenon, argon and krypton in it than in the Sun. Jupiter also has 67 satellites, some of which are quite similar in size to planets. For example, Ganymede is 8% larger than Mercury, and Io has its own atmosphere. There is also a theory that Jupiter was supposed to become a full-fledged star, but at the stage of development it remained a planet.

- 4th in terms of luminosity : In terms of luminosity, the planet is ahead of the Sun, Moon and Venus. One of the five planets that can be found without tools.

- The earliest records belong to the Babulonians : Jupiter is mentioned as early as the 7th-8th centuries. BEFORE CHRIST. Received a name in honor of the supreme deity of the pantheon (of the Greeks - Zeus). In Mesopotamia it was Marduk, and among the Germanic tribes it was Thor.

- On shortest day : Performs an axial rotation in just 9 hours and 55 minutes. Due to the rapid rotation, a flattening at the poles and an expansion of the equatorial line occurs.

- A year lasts 11.8 years : From the point of view of terrestrial observation, its movement seems unbelievably slow.

-There are some remarkable cloud formations : The upper atmospheric layer is divided into cloud belts and zones. Represented by crystals of ammonia, sulfur and their mixtures.

-It's the biggest storm : Images capture the big red spot - a large-scale storm that hasn't stopped for over 50 years. He is so huge that he can swallow three Earths.

-The structure includes compounds of stone, metal, and hydrogen : Under the atmospheric layer are layers of gaseous and liquid hydrogen, as well as a nucleus of ice, stone and metals.

-Ganymede is the largest satellite in the system : Among the satellites, the largest are Ganymede, Callisto, Io and Europa. The first in diameter covers 5,268 km, which is larger than Mercury.

-There is a ringing system : The rings are thin and are represented by particles of dust ejected by moons in collisions with comets or asteroids. They start at a distance of 92,000 km and extend as far as 225,000 km from Jupiter. Thickness - 2000-12500 km.

- 8 missions sent : These are Pioneers 10 and 11, Voyagers 1 and 2, Galileo, Cassini, Willis and New Horizons. Futures can focus on satellites.

Saturn

Saturn is the sixth planet from the Sun and, possibly, the most beautiful object of the Solar system . The second largest planet in the solar system, like Jupiter, belongs to the gas giants .

This is the most distant planet from the star, which can be found from the Earth without using a telescope or binoculars. So what about her existence is known for a long time. In front of you is one of the four gas giants, located 6th in order from the Sun. We will be curious to find out what the plan of Saturn is, but first have a look at interesting facts about the plan of Saturn.

Saturn can be found without the use of televisions, therefore it was seen by other ancient people. Mentions are found in legends and mythology. The best recording of the recording is assigned to Bavilon, where the plan was treated with a link to the knowledge of the zodiac. The ancient Greeks called this giant Kronoc, who was a god of charity and was the youngest of the Titans. Then I was able to calculate the orbital passage of Saturn, when the planet was in opposition.

In Pime, they used a Greek tradition and gave the present name. In ancient Hebrew, the planet was called Shabbatai, and in the Ocmani Empire - Zuhal. The Indians have Shani, who judges all, evaluating good and good deeds.

The Chinese and Japanese called him an earth star, considering one of the elements. But the plan was observed only in 1610, when Galileo saw her in his telecopy and provided a ring. But the scientist thought that these are two satellites. Only Christian Huygens corrected the error. He also found Titan, and Giovanni Caccini - Iapetus, Pea, Tefia and Dione. The next important step was taken by William Herschel in 1789, when he found Mimac and Enceladus. And in 1848 Hyperion appears.

Phoebus in 1899 found William Pickering, who guessed that the satellite had an irregular orbital and rotated synchronously with the planet. In the 20th century, it became clear that Titan had a dense atmosphere that had not been seen before. Planeta Saturn is an interesting object for research. At our site, you can study his photo, get acquainted with the video on the planet and learn many more interesting facts. Below is the map of the Saturn.

About 96% of the planet's chemical composition is hydrogen. Saturn stands out for its rings. There are also other giant planets, but Saturn has the most noticeable ones. The rings are not a single whole, but consist of trillions of small bodies orbiting Saturn. In total, scientists distinguish 4 rings of Saturn, the thickness of which does not exceed a kilometer. The largest moon of Saturn is Titan, which is larger than Mercury. It has been proven that there is liquid on its surface - lakes of methane and other hydrocarbons.

- Can be found without tools : Saturn is the 5th brightest in the solar system, so you can see it through binoculars or a telescope.

- The ancients saw him : The Babulonians and the inhabitants of the Far East were also watching him. Named after the Roman titan (analogue of the Greek Kronos).

- The flattest planet : The polar diameter covers 90% of the equatorial diameter, based on low density and rapid rotation. The planet performs an axial revolution every 10 hours and 34 minutes.

- A year lasts 29.4 years : The ancient Assurians, because of their slowness, called the planet "Lubadshagush" - "the oldest of the oldest".

- There are ridges in the upper atmosphere : The composition of the upper atmosphere is represented by ammoniacal ice. There are clouds of water below them, then there are cold mixtures of hydrogen and sulfur.

- Oval thunderstorms present : The area above the North Pole has taken on a hexagonal shape (hexagon). Researchers believe it could be a wave pattern in upper clouds. There is also a hurricane-like vortex over the South Pole.

- The planet is represented mainly by hydrogen. The planet is divided into layers, which penetrate more densely into Saturn. At great depths, hydrogen turns metallic. It is based on a warm interior.

- With the best ring system : Saturn's rings are made of shards of ice and a small amount of carbon dust. They extend over 120,700 km, but incredibly thin - 20 m.

- The lunar family includes 62 satellites : Saturn's moons are frozen worlds. The biggest are Titan and Rhea. Enceladus may have an ocean below the surface.

- Titanium has a complex nitrogen atmosphere : Consists of ice and stone. The frozen surface layer is endowed with lakes of liquid methane and landfills covered with frozen nitrogen. Can have life.

- Sent 4 missions : These are Pioneer 11, Voyager 1 and 2 and Cassini-Huygens.

Uranus

The first six planets of the solar system have been known to mankind since prehistoric times. Uranus, on the other hand, became the first planet that was actually discovered. This was done by William Herschel in 1781. The planet's axis of rotation is tilted at 98 °, because of this, sunlight is distributed extremely unevenly. Each pole of Uranus is continuously illuminated by the Sun for 42 years, and then plunges into darkness for 42 years. Uranus is a special type of ice giant. In fact, it is a gas giant with a large amount of ice in its atmosphere. Of particular interest to astronomers is the satellite of Uranus Enceladus. It is covered with a crust of ice, under which the water ocean is located. It is assumed that extraterrestrial life may exist in it.

Uranus is included in the list of five planets, which could have been seen with the unaided eye. But this is a dull object, and the orbital path passes too slowly, so the ancient people believed that there was a classy star ahead of them. This review is given to Hippaphus, who pointed to the body as a star in 128 BC. e. The first accurate observation of the plan was performed by John Flamstid in 1690. He noticed it at least 6 times and recorded it as a star (34 Taurus).

Approximately 20 times behind Uranium was tracked by Pierre Lemonier in 1750-1769. But it wasn't until 1781 that William Herschel began to observe Uranus as a planet. Of course, he himself believed that he was looking at a comet, which in its habits resembles a planetary object. As a result, other astronomers joined the study, including Anders Lexell. It was the first to determine an almost circular orbit. This was confirmed by Johann Bode. In 1783, Uranus was officially recognized as a planet and Herschel received 200 pounds from the king.

For this, the scientist nicknamed the object the Star of George in honor of the new patron. But the name did not come out of the UK. The modern name was suggested by Johann Bode. It was the Latin version of the Greek god of the sky. The name stuck and became official in 1850. Below is a map of Uranus. Its radius is 25267 km. The temperature on Uranus is kept at -230 degrees Celsius, making it the coldest planet. It also has a unique feature: the axis of rotation is located at an angle, which is why, when moving, the planet looks like a rolling ball. The surface is predominantly ice, with small amounts of helium and hydrogen.

Uranus , with a mass 14 times that of Earth, is the lightest of the giant planets. The peculiarity of this planet, which appears to the observer in shades of blue-green, is in its rotation. The axis of rotation of the planet is practically parallel to the plane of the ecliptic. In ordinary language, Uranus lies on its side. While other planets can be compared to spinning tops, Uranus is more like a rolling ball. But this did not stop him from acquiring 13 rings and 27 satellites, the most famous of which are Oberon, Titania, Ariel, Umbriel. It has a much colder core than other gas giants and radiates very little heat into space.

- Discovered by William Herschel in 1781 : It is a dark planet, therefore inaccessible to the ancients. At first, Herschel thought he saw a comet, but after a few years the object was given planetary status. The scientist wanted to call him "George's Star", but Johann Bode's version improved.

- Axial rotation takes 17 hours and 14 minutes : The planet Uranus is characterized by retrograde, which does not converge with the general direction.

-The year lasts 84 years : But some areas are directed directly towards the Sun and so it lasts about 42 years. The rest of the time is spent in darkness.

- It is an ice giant : Like the rest of the gas giant, the upper layer of Uranus is made up of hydrogen and helium. But underneath is a mantle of ice centered on ice and a boulder. The upper atmosphere is made up of crystals of water ice, ammonia and methane. Icy planet With a temperature of -224 ° C, it is considered the coldest planet. Periodically, Neptune cools even more, but Uranus freezes most of the time. The upper atmospheric layer is covered with a methane haze that hides storms.

- There are two sets of thin rings : The particles are extremely small. There are 11 inner rings and 2 outer rings.

Formed during the collapse of old satellites. The first rings were noticed only in 1977, and the rest - in the images of the Hubble Telescope in 2003-2005.

- The moons are named after literary figures : All of the moons of Uranus are named after the characters of William Shakespeare and Alexander Pope. The most interesting is Miranda with icy cannouons and a strange surface.

- We sent a mission : Voyager 2 visited Uranus in 1986 at a distance of 81,500 km.

Neptune

The eighth planet from the Sun was discovered not through observations, but through mathematical calculations. Observing anomalies in the movement of Uranus, scientists have put forward the assumption that they arose due to the presence of another large celestial body. Neptune has a radius of 24,547 km. The surface is similar to uranium, but the strongest winds in the system are walking on it, accelerating to 260 m / s.

It was discovered using mathematical calculations. A study of the orbit of Uranus showed that there must be a massive celestial body behind it, distorting its orbit. In 1845-1846 the Frenchman Le Verrier calculated the orbit of an unknown planet, after which Halle was able to find Neptune using telescopes. In its composition, Neptune is similar to Uranus, it also belongs to the class of ice giants. In the atmosphere of the planet, the strongest winds rage in the entire solar system, reaching 2100 km / h. The reason for this weather is an internal source of heat, whose nature is not clear to scientists. However, Neptune gives off 2.5 times more heat into space than it receives from the Sun.

The Neptune was not fixed until the 19th century. Although, if you carefully look at Galileo's stocks from 1612, you can note that the points lead to the position of the ice giant. So they just took the plan for a star. In 1821, Alexis Bouvard published schemes reflecting the orbital path of Uranus. But the further review showed deviations from the drawing, so the scientist thought that there was a large body nearby, influencing the path. John Adams began a detailed study of Uranus' orbital passage in 1843. Independently of him in the years 1845-1846. worked by Urbe Le Verrier. He shared his knowledge with Johann Halle at the Berlin Observatory. The latter confirmed that there was something big nearby.

The discovery of the planet Neptune caused much controversy regarding the discoverer. But the scientific world has recognized the merits of Le Verrier and Adams. But in 1998, the former was considered to be doing more. At first, Le Verrier suggested naming the object after itself, which caused a lot of outrage. But its second sentence (Neptune) has become the modern name. The point is, it fits into the naming tradition. Below is a map of Neptune.

Outwardly, Neptune is similar to Uranus; its spectrum is also dominated by the bands of methane and hydrogen. The heat flux from Neptune significantly exceeds the power of the sun's heat falling on it, which indicates the existence of an internal source of energy. It is possible that much of the internal heat is generated by the tides caused by the massive moon Triton, which revolves in the opposite direction at a distance of 14.5 of the planet's radius. Voyager 2, flying in 1989 at a distance of 5000 km from the cloud layer, discovered 6 more satellites and 5 rings near Neptune. The Great Dark Spot and a complex system of vortex flows were discovered in the atmosphere. Triton's pinkish surface reveals amazing geological features, including powerful geysers. The Proteus satellite discovered by Voyager turned out to be larger than Nereid, discovered from Earth back in 1949.

- The ancients did not know about him : Neptune cannot be found without the use of tools. It was not noticed for the first time until 1846. The position was calculated mathematically. The name was given in honor of the sea deity among the Romans.

- Rotates rapidly on an axis : Equatorial clouds complete one revolution in 18 hours.

- The smallest among the ice giants : He is smaller than Uranus, but larger in mass. The heavy atmosphere hides layers of hydrogen, helium and methane. There is water, ammonia and methane ice. The internal node is represented by a rock.

- The atmosphere is filled with hydrogen, helium and methane: Neptune's methane absorbs red, so the planet looks blue. The high clouds are constantly drifting.

- Active climate : It should be noted the major storms and strong winds. One of the large-scale storms was recorded in 1989 - the Great Dark Spot, which lasted for 5 years.

- There are thin rings : represented by particles of ice mixed with grains of dust and carbonaceous matter.

- There are 14 satellites : Neptune's most interesting satellite is Triton, a frozen world that releases particles of nitrogen and dust below the surface. May be attracted to planetary gravity.

- We sent a mission : In 1989, Voyager 2 flew over Neptune, sending the first large-scale images of the system. The Hubble Telescope also observed the planet.

Printed in Great Britain
by Amazon